# Johnstown Flood

## Other titles in the *American Disasters* series:

# Johnstown Flood

## The Day the Dam Burst

Mary Gow

AMERICAN DISASTERS

**Enslow Publishers, Inc.**

40 Industrial Road        PO Box 38

Box 398                 Aldershot

Berkeley Heights, NJ 07922   Hants GU12 6BP

USA                            UK

http://www.enslow.com

*To Emily*

**Library of Congress Cataloging-in-Publication Data**

Gow, Mary.
    Johnstown flood : the day the dam burst / Mary Gow.
        p. cm. — (American disasters)
    Includes bibliographical references (p. ) and index.
    Summary: An account of the great Johnstown, Pennsylvania, flood of 1889,
when a dam failed and over two thousand people died, making this one of the
worst peacetime disasters in the history of the United States.
    ISBN 0-7660-2109-2
    1. Floods—Pennsylvania—Johnstown—History—19th century—Juvenile litera-
ture. 2. Johnstown (Pa.)—History—19th century—Juvenile literature.
[1. Floods—Pennsylvania—Johnstown. 2. Johnstown (Pa.)—History—19th
century.] I. Title. II. Series.
F159.J7 G69   2003
974.8'77—dc21

                                           2002005498

Printed in the United States of America

10 9 8 7 6 5 4 3 2 1

The author would like to thank Robin Rummel and everyone at the Johnstown Area
Heritage Association for the assistance they provided during the course of her research
for this book.

**Illustration Credits:** Courtesy of Johnstown Area Heritage Association
Archives, pp. 1, 6, 12, 24, 27, 29, 31, 35; Courtesy of Johnstown Area Heritage
Association Archives, Louis S. Semple Clarke Collection, p. 16; Courtesy of
Steven Hewitt, pp. 9, 13, 15, 19, 26, 34, 39, 41, 42; Courtesy of the Johnstown
Tribune-Democrat, p. 40; National Archives, p. 33.

**Cover Illustration:** Courtesy of the Johnstown Tribune-Democrat.

# Contents

This photograph of six-year-old Gertrude Quinn was taken from her book, *Johnstown and its Flood*.

# CHAPTER 1

# A Dangerous Proposition

Gertrude Quinn's feet were wet again. She knew that she was supposed to stay inside, out of the rain, but she could not resist the unusual sights outdoors. Water was flowing across the lawn in front of her house. Ducklings that belonged to her brother, Vincent, splashed in the yard. Purple pansies in the flower bed floated up and down like tiny lily pads. Six-year-old Gertrude sat on the edge of the porch and dangled her feet in the floodwater.[1]

Water had been creeping up the streets of Johnstown, Pennsylvania, since early morning on that Friday, May 31, 1889. The rain had started the previous afternoon, after the Memorial Day parade. Civil War veterans marched in the celebration. Bands played and crowds cheered. At first, the rain fell like a gentle mist.

During the night, the drizzle turned to a downpour. Torrents pounded down on Johnstown and the surrounding Allegheny Mountains. Tiny streams and mountain rivers swelled and began to overflow their banks.

Johnstown saw occasional floods. Yet, this storm and this flood seemed more ominous to some people. Gertrude's father, James Quinn, worried. Fifteen miles upstream from Johnstown, on the south fork of the Little Conemaugh River, a dam was built. The massive earthen dam held back a reservoir—a sizable lake, high in the mountains. That dam troubled Quinn.

"I have seen the dam," Quinn told Gertrude's aunt, Abbie Geis, who was visiting from Kansas. "It is a mighty body of water at any time; and now I feel with continuous rain, it is a very dangerous proposition for the people of Johnstown." He said that if the dam broke, not a brick would still stand in Johnstown. Geis laughed at his concern.

"James, you are too anxious," she said.[2]

School was closed that day because of the high water. Gertrude and three of her sisters were at home. Gertrude's mother was out of town. Abbie Geis and Libby Hipp, the Quinn's nursemaid, were caring for the children.

Although he was worried, James Quinn went to his store, "Geis, Foster and Quinn," one of grandest stores in Johnstown. When he went to work, Quinn told Geis and Hipp not to let the children outside. If the flood got worse he would come home, he said. He would then take them up the hill at the end of town to be safe above the water.

Vincent Quinn, a teenager, was allowed outside. He splashed in the streets like other boys. In the afternoon, as the rain continued to fall, Vincent went to help his Uncle Louie in town.

A few blocks away, water was knee-deep on

The slope in the foreground and hill in the background are where the 930-foot-long, 70-foot-high South Fork Dam once stood. The railroad line and South Fork stream now run through the low spot.

Washington Street in front of the Heisers' store. George and Mathilde Heiser and their sixteen-year-old son, Victor, lived upstairs, over the store.

The Heisers' store opened that morning, but the water slowed business. By mid-afternoon, few people were shopping. The Heisers went upstairs. George Heiser saw that the water was almost into their barn. He asked Victor to untie the horses. If the water rose too high, the horses would struggle in their stalls. They would be safer untied. Victor left his socks and shoes in the house. Barefoot, he waded over to the barn.[3]

As Gertrude watched her pansies, Vincent helped his

uncle, and Victor untied the horses, catastrophe was already devastating towns upriver. Destruction raced toward Johnstown from the South Fork Dam.

James Quinn came home from the store just before 4:00 P.M. He knew it was time to flee. Suddenly, the Quinns heard a roar. Victor Heiser, standing in his barn, heard it too. Everyone in Johnstown heard it before they saw it. The sound, Quinn later said, froze the marrow in his bones.[4]

"Run for your lives. Follow me straight to the hill," Quinn commanded. He grabbed the baby and headed out the door with Gertrude's two other sisters at his sides. Libby Hipp carried Gertrude.

"Follow me. Don't stop for anything," Quinn ordered the others.[5] They followed him out of the house and started down the porch stairs. Quinn charged into the watery street.

Abbie Geis paused on the steps. "I don't like to put my feet into that dirty water," she said. "We may catch cold, get sick and die."

"What shall we do?" Hipp asked, terrified.

"Lets run to the third floor. This big house will never move," replied Geis. Hipp held Gertrude, who was kicking and screaming. Together, they flew up the stairs.[6]

# CHAPTER 2

# The Dam in the Mountains

**W**ater was always important to Johnstown. The city was almost surrounded by it. The Little Conemaugh and the Sandy Creek Rivers rush down steep slopes of the Allegheny Mountains. Like the branches of a "Y," they meet to become the Conemaugh River. Johnstown was founded in the low, flat, triangular piece of land in the middle of the "Y."

Johnstown's location on the rivers helped it grow. In the 1800s, river valleys provided travel routes through the craggy terrain of the Allegheny Mountains. Canals and railroads were built in the valleys. In 1831, the Main Line Canal opened, connecting Johnstown to Pittsburgh. Johnstown settlers built barges and started businesses floating iron ore and lumber to Pittsburgh. In 1854, the Pennsylvania Railroad reached Johnstown. The town was connected to the world.

After the railroad came, steel mills opened along Johnstown's rivers. From the surrounding mountains,

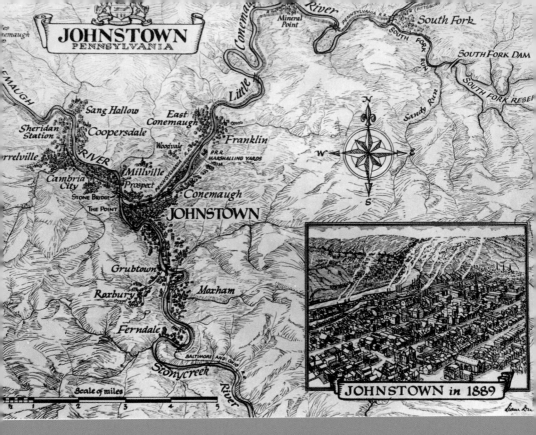

This map shows Johnstown and the surrounding
boroughs. The South fork Dam, fifteen miles upstream,
is shown in the upper right corner.

iron ore was mined and forged into rails, plows and wire.
The mills thrived and the little city grew. In 1889, Cambria
Iron Company mills stretched for miles along Johnstown's
riverbanks. Seven thousand workers were on the company's payroll. Dozens of stores, hundreds of houses,
hotels, saloons, banks, offices, a theater, and a roller-
skating rink stood in town. Twenty-six churches and
twenty schools served the community.

Back in 1843, before the steel mills, the State of
Pennsylvania started building a dam fifteen miles

upstream from Johnstown. The reservoir of water behind the dam was intended to fill canals.

And what a dam! Longer than three football fields, the crest of the South Fork Dam stretched 930 feet across. It was seventy-two feet high, about the same as a seven-story building. On the outside the dam looked like a pile of rocks. Inside, it was made of layers of earth and clay carefully packed together.[1]

The reservoir was eventually named Lake Conemaugh. Some people said it was the largest man-made lake in the world, but it was not. Still, Lake

*A*t two miles long and about one-half mile wide, Lake Conemaugh once filled this valley. The town of St. Michaels now occupies the land. Coal trains like the one above often pass through the former lake bed.

Conemaugh was big. It was about two miles long and a half mile across.

Pipes that ran through the dam could be opened and closed like faucets. This was important for safety. If there were leaks in the dam, the water behind it could be drained. For added safety, a spillway was cut through mountain rock around the dam. If water got too high, it could flow out through the spillway without eroding the dam.

In 1852, the dam was finished. Two years later, it no longer had a reason to exist. The canals were going out of business. Railroads had taken their place.

Like a big shimmering bowl of water, Lake Conemaugh lay quietly high in the mountains. Local people sometimes fished there, but the lake was largely ignored.

In a heavy rainstorm in 1862, water leaked through part of the dam. A watchman opened the discharge pipes and let water out. Part of the dam collapsed anyway. Little damage occurred downstream because the pipes released most of the water slowly.[2] After the collapse, the reservoir could not be filled. Water flowed through a low spot in the dam. Lake Conemaugh became more a puddle than a lake.

In 1879, new life came to the mountains. Benjamin Ruff bought the dam and Lake Conemaugh to start a private club. He named it "The South Fork Hunting and Fishing Club." The club was a mountaintop retreat for some of Pennsylvania's wealthiest men. Andrew Carnegie, Henry Clay Frick, Andrew Mellon, and other Pittsburgh millionaires bought shares in the club. Members had fortunes made in steel, railroads, banking, construction, coal, and other businesses. Benjamin Ruff was the club's first president.

Once the club was established, changes followed. The members wanted a lovely big lake, not a shallow little puddle. The dam needed to be repaired. Ruff did not hire an engineer to supervise the repairs. An engineer is a person trained in the design and construction of large building projects like bridges, roads, and dams. Without expert advice, workmen filled the hole in the dam with stones and branches. They packed manure, hay, and

*I*n 1889, the clubhouse dining room of the South Fork Hunting and Fishing Club seated 150 people. Upstairs were forty-seven guest rooms for the members.

brush around the fill. Men who watched the repairs always remembered how poorly the work was done.[3]

Ruff disregarded another important part of the dam. The discharge pipes had been removed before his purchase. Ruff did not replace the pipes. Finally, the top few feet of the dam were removed. Lower, it was also wider. The club put a scenic carriage road across its crest.

Ruff's repairs were finished and Lake Conemaugh was filled. The members of the club liked to fish. Trout flourished in the mountain streams. The members wanted lake

Cottages of club members overlooked Lake Conemaugh and the boathouses. Some of the cottages had as many as seventeen bedrooms.

fish, too. They imported 1,000 black bass from Lake Erie. The fish cost the club about $1,000.[4] The members did not want their expensive fish to get away. They installed iron screens around the spillway to keep the fish from swimming downstream.

Some club members stayed in the guest rooms in the clubhouse; others built cottages. The cottages had wide porches, towers, and as many as seventeen bedrooms. On their sparkling lake, the club kept a fleet of boats. They had two steam yachts, fifty canoes, sailboats, and rowboats.

The club members were secretive about their summers on the mountain. Groundskeepers chased away curious local people. Downstream, some Johnstown residents worried about the big dam. Most people, however, did not. It was unthinkable that the dam could fail, especially since it was owned by such wealthy men.

Daniel Morrell, the man in charge of Cambria Iron Company, Johnstown's biggest industry, thought disaster could happen. Morrell sent his engineer, John Fulton, to look at the South Fork Dam. Fulton did not like what he saw. He reported back to Morrell and sent a letter to Benjamin Ruff. Fulton was alarmed that there were no discharge pipes. He also considered Ruff's repairs shoddy. Fulton was afraid that the dam could fail.[5]

Benjamin Ruff wrote back. His letter was almost insulting. He thought Fulton's criticism was petty. Ruff ended by saying, "You and your people are in no danger from our enterprise."[6]

# CHAPTER 3

# Prepare for the Worst

The storm that started on Memorial Day, 1889, became fierce through the night. Rain slammed down on the mountains. Sheets of water flowed across the land. The storm pounded on roofs and windows. Streams began to overflow their banks.

John Parke, Jr., woke up on Friday morning in the South Fork clubhouse. He was alarmed to see that Lake Conemaugh had risen two feet overnight. Parke was a distinguished young man who studied engineering at the University of Pennsylvania. At the South Fork Hunting and Fishing Club, he supervised repairs and building projects. Parke realized that Lake Conemaugh was rising quickly.

On horseback, Parke rode from the clubhouse to the dam. Colonel Elias Unger, the club's current president, was already there. Workmen were shoveling dirt on the dam to try to make it higher.[1]

Lake Conemaugh's surface was near the top of the

*U*nlike the other members of the South Fork Hunting and Fishing Club, Colonel Unger lived in this farmhouse, away from other Club buildings. His house overlooked the dam and lake.

dam. Branches clogged the fish screens and blocked the spillway. When Colonel Unger finally allowed the workmen to remove the screens, it was too late. The screens would not budge. The lake inched higher and higher.

Parke saw that disaster was approaching. Just before noon, he rode his horse downstream to the town of South Fork to telegraph a warning to Johnstown.

The message said something like this: "South Fork Dam is liable to break: Notify people to prepare for the worst."[2] The telegraph arrived in Johnstown, but no alarm was sounded.

There had been rumors about the dam before, but disaster had never followed. "The dam is becoming dangerous and may possibly go," read a second telegraph. It arrived in Johnstown at about 2:45 P.M. Lake Conemaugh had begun to pour over the center of the dam. At 3:15 P.M., the South Fork Dam burst.

"The whole dam seemed to push out all at once," said Ed Schwartzentruver, who was there. "No, not a break, just one big push."[3]

As much water as flows over Niagara Fall in thirty-six minutes, plunged down the valley all at once.[4] The water in Lake Conemaugh weighed about 40 billion pounds.

Some witnesses described it as a wall of water, others as a great grinding ball. What people saw first was the front of an enormous wave. In narrow spots, the wave rose up to seventy-five feet high. Most of the way its height was between twenty and forty feet. This mountain of water tore down the valley. It rolled as fast as forty miles per hour.

First, the water reached South Fork. Most of the town stood on the hillside above the river. Townspeople watched their bridge, mill, and twenty buildings disappear below them.

Next was Mineral Point. Houses, barns, fences, telegraph poles, farm animals, and streets were stripped from the earth. Sixteen people had been killed at that point.

Work Train Number Two was on the tracks outside of East Conemaugh. "We didn't see it, but we heard the noise of it coming," said John Hess, the train's engineer.

"It was like a hurricane through wooded country."[5] Hess opened the locomotive's whistle to scream out a warning. Work Train Number Two raced down the tracks. Everyone who heard the shriek of Hess's whistle knew something was disastrously wrong.

Freight cars, passenger trains, and locomotives sat on the tracks in the railroad yards in East Conemaugh. At the sound of John Hess's whistle, passengers and railroad workers fled. They clamored over the tracks and up the hill. Trains were nothing to the advancing wave. Locomotives that weighed more than 170,000 pounds were snatched up by the flood. Hundreds of railroad cars were swept away.

Then it was Woodvale's turn. Mills, including the wireworks, stood in Woodvale. Nearly one thousand people lived in town. After the wave passed, not one house was still standing. Only nine or ten local families did not lose a parent or child to the disaster. Miles of Woodvale's barbed wire disappeared into the raging flood.

After Woodvale, Johnstown was next.

# CHAPTER 4

# "The End of the World"

**W**hen Victor Heiser heard the roar he looked over at his house from the barn. His parents waved frantically from the upstairs window. They gestured to him to climb to the barn's roof. Victor scrambled up through a trapdoor. From the roof he saw the flood wave. So many houses, trees, dead animals, railroad cars, and shattered pieces of lumber churned in it that it did not even look like water.

The flood tore into Johnstown with unimaginable violence. It was 4:08 P.M. A furious sea of water and debris blasted through and over everything. The flood was deeper than many houses were tall.

The flood wave struck Victor's home with his parents still inside. In a blink, the house was gone. Next, the wave slammed into the barn. Instead of shattering, the barn began to roll. It tumbled over and over. Victor scrambled to stay on top. Suddenly, the house of his neighbors, the Fenns, was in his path. Victor jumped to the Fenns' roof.

He grabbed its edge as the wall below him collapsed. Victor's hands could not hold him for long and he fell toward the water. He landed on a floating chunk of his own barn.[1]

People clutched anything that floated, trying to stay on top of the swirling, thrashing flood. Mrs. Fenn rode past Victor on a barrel. Her seven children were nowhere to be seen.

The flood struck the steep slopes that surrounded Johnstown. The water bounded back in another wave of destruction. Currents threw victims one way and then another. A sturdy stone railroad bridge crossed the Conemaugh River just below town. Seven solid low arches stood in the riverbed under the tracks. It was a strong bridge designed to carry heavily loaded trains. At first, the bridge and its arches slowed the flood's downstream surge. Later, the bridge added to Johnstown's nightmare.

Abbie Geis, Libby Hipp, and Gertrude made it to the third floor of the Quinn's house just before the wave hit. At the top of the steps, they looked out the window. Water-filled streets were teeming with terrified people pushing toward the hill. Many dragged their children and pets with them.

"Libby, this is the end of the world," said Geis.[2]

Geis and Hipp pulled Gertrude into a closet with them. The house swayed, then lurched back and forth. Plaster and dust fell from the ceiling. The floor opened. Water rushed over their heads.

Everything was dark and Gertrude was in the water.

**T**hese two photos show the center of Johnstown before the flood (above) and after (below).

Geis and Hipp were gone. Sticks and filthy water filled Gertrude's mouth. Crying and trying to spit out the water, she saw a bit of light, a hole to the outdoors. Gertrude climbed through it to daylight. Her mother's mattress floated on some wooden debris. Gertrude crawled aboard.[3]

Gertrude tipped and tilted. The mattress was tossed by the raging water. It collided with a dead horse but bounced past it.

A big roof carrying about twenty people floated by. Gertrude cried out for help. One man, Max McAchren, leapt from the roof and swam to her. McAchren climbed on the mattress and steadied it. Gertrude clung to his neck.

The roof drifted a little further. Struck by debris, it began to spin, then it sank. Some of the people stayed afloat but most disappeared.

Max McAchren and Gertrude Quinn floated through the pandemonium together. Eventually they drifted near a house at the edge of town. Two men were pulling people to safety with a pole. They were not close enough to reach Gertrude's mattress.

"Throw that baby over here to us," one man called out.

"Do you think you can catch her?" asked McAchren.

"We can try," he shouted.[4]

Max McAchren, a powerful man, picked up Gertrude and threw her. She flew nearly fifteen feet through the air.

Not far away, Victor Heiser climbed off his raft to join

*T*he stone railroad bridge was built in the early 1880s. It is located directly below "the Point"—the spot in Johnstown where the Little Conemaugh and Sandy Run Rivers meet.

survivors on the roof of another house. Johnstown was demolished in ten minutes. The worst violence of the flood was over quickly, but the city still was not safe. The few remaining buildings were undermined by the flood's force. Water and mud were everywhere and still too deep to cross. Survivors could not leave the houses or treetops where they had found temporary safety. Through the night, buildings collapsed, often crushing people huddled inside them.

At the stone bridge, a new horror started. Thirty acres of flood debris—trees, splintered houses, furniture, and bodies—had jammed up behind the bridge. The debris

*T*his popular print of the time shows the flood colliding into the stone bridge. People clung to the roofs of their homes as they were swept away by the raging waters of the great flood.

caught fire, perhaps from stoves or lanterns burning in mangled houses. People were trapped in the wreckage. About sixty people died in the fires.

All night, survivors waited sleeplessly for morning. No one knew who or what was left of their former lives. In the morning, they looked out on utter desolation.

Before the flood, approximately 25,000 people lived in and around Johnstown. Now, the city was gone and one tenth of its population was dead. Mud, shattered buildings, and bodies lay where streets and homes stood the day before; 1,600 houses and 260 businesses were demolished.

The people of Johnstown were stunned, hungry, and

homeless. Many had only the soaking clothes on their backs. There was no drinking water and no food. The only shelter was on the hillsides. Injured and trapped survivors needed to be rescued. The dead needed to be buried.

Victor Heiser had spent the night in the house where he landed. In the morning, he slogged through mud and rafted over water to reach solid ground.

"Everyone I met was on the same sad errand—looking for parents, children, relatives, or friends," he later wrote. "Bodies were already being taken out of the ruins."[5]

The flood's toll was horrific: 2,209 people died. Every living person in Johnstown had lost someone.[6]

George and Mathilde Heiser, Abbie Geis, Libby Hipp, and Vincent Quinn all perished in the flood. Stories were heart-wrenching. Anna Fenn, whom Victor saw astride the barrel, lost her husband and all seven of her children. The entire Fisher family, both parents and six children, died together. They were found locked in each other's arms. William Huffman, a popular tailor, drowned. Twenty-nine of his relatives, including his wife and most of his children, died too.[7]

Altogether, ninety-nine whole families perished. With the tragedies, there were also stories of heroes like Max McAchren. Because of McAchren's mighty throw, Gertrude landed safely. Soaking and shivering, she was wrapped in blankets and carried up the hill to the home of a Mrs. Metz. Other survivors were also sheltered in the Metz home. McAchren himself was later rescued as well.

Gertrude's father, James Quinn, and her sisters spent

the night in another hillside house. On Saturday morning, Quinn was shaving when he heard that Gertrude was alive. His face covered in lather, he ran to find her.

When Quinn reached the Metz house, Gertrude saw him. She ran outside and into his arms. Strangers in the street watched them and wept with joy.[8]

Thirty acres of wreckage piled up behind the arches of the stone railroad bridge that crossed the Conemaugh River. Houses, trees, bodies, and furniture were smashed together. In fact, much clearing had been done by the time this photograph was taken.

# CHAPTER 5

# Relief and Recovery

The Johnstown Flood of 1889 was one of the worst peacetime disasters in the history of the United States. The wall of water that plunged down the narrow valley of the Little Conemaugh River that day crushed houses like eggshells, threw railroad cars from their tracks, and tore trees from the earth. The force of the water destroyed the town and took the lives of more than 2,000 people.

Saturday morning, farmers from the surrounding hillsides arrived. Their wagons were full of food and milk. When the farmers saw Johnstown, they gave the survivors everything. Then, they went back to their farms and brought more.

Newspaper reporters reached Johnstown as the floodwater receded. Telegraph wires were strung, and news of the tragedy reached the world. The Johnstown Flood was the biggest news story of the century after the assassination of President Abraham Lincoln.

Early accounts of the disaster had reached Pittsburgh

late Friday night. Emergency meetings were held. Trains with bedding, tents, clothing, food, medicine, and bandages started for Johnstown on Saturday afternoon. The trains ran as far as the tracks still stood. Men carried the supplies the final miles.

One of the early messages to Johnstown asked how many doctors to send. "Physicians are not needed. Send as many undertakers as possible," was the reply.[1]

There were many injuries, but far more deaths.

*T*his jumble of houses was tossed together by the flood. Their roofs provided a good perch for viewing the area and a place to be photographed.

Undertakers from near and far went to help. They were followed by coffins—eleven boxcars carried only coffins.

In spite of their despair, Johnstown residents helped themselves and helped each other. Saturday afternoon, less than twenty-four hours after the flood, they held a big public meeting. Survivors organized into committees. They opened temporary morgues for the dead. Volunteers formed search teams, supply groups, and a police force.

Rescuers freed many people trapped at the stone bridge. Men climbed through the wreckage moving logs and debris to free anyone they could save. Rescues were greeted with great fanfare.

Animals were saved, too. Volunteers found a half-drowned cat. They named him "Flood Tim," and kept him as their pet. A black rabbit was returned to a little boy. A horse, buried to its shoulders, survived.

Screams led volunteers to the attic of a damaged home. Inside, they found a very agitated parrot. It stomped around the floor, shrieking that it had "a devil of a time."[2]

People poured into Johnstown to help—6,000 arrived in the first week. Firemen from Pittsburgh put out the fire at the bridge. Lumberjacks cut up debris. Railroad workers laid tracks. The State of Pennsylvania sent soldiers and General Daniel Hartman Hastings. General Hastings was in charge of coordinating the relief effort. He was greatly respected and appreciated in Johnstown.

Clara Barton, founder of the American Red Cross, arrived five days after the flood. She organized temporary housing. Five Red Cross hotels were built to provide shelter and meals.

Trainloads of donations poured into Johnstown. Cincinnati sent 20,000 pounds of ham. Indianapolis sent 11,000 loaves of bread. Detroit sent 30 dozen chairs. Lumber companies sent lumber. Hardware stores sent nails. Pillowcases, sheets, and children's clothes arrived. Housewives sent groceries. Altogether, it was estimated that Johnstown received more than 1,400 railroad cars full of supplies.

Clara Barton, founder of the American Red Cross, arrived in Johnstown several days after the flood to help organize temporary housing and arrange meals for flood victims.

Money was also given. A total of $3,742,818 was donated to Johnstown's relief. With the world's generosity and their own determination, Johnstown residents had the tools to rebuild their lives and their city.

Everywhere, people cleaned up. Bodies were buried every day for weeks. Carcasses of animals were cremated to prevent contagious diseases.

Slowly, in the midst of the misery, a kind of excitement crept into the city's mood. Thousands of people were in Johnstown. The railroad lines were rebuilt. Daily trains brought supplies. The debris at the stone bridge was blasted out with dynamite. Commissaries distributed food and clothing. The saloons—which were all gone anyway—were replaced by lemonade stands. (Alcoholic drinks were not allowed in town for about a month.)

Sightseers came to look at the devastation. Soldiers dug out streets and basements. The Cambria Iron Company announced that mills would reopen. Workers still had jobs and would be paid. Johnstown would rebuild.

"Why did this tragedy happen?" residents began to wonder. They remembered concerns about the dam. They

*O*n March 31, 1892, a monument and plot was dedicated at the Grandview Cemetery for the unknown dead. Seven hundred and seventy-seven identical white stones were erected and dedicated.

The Schultz House was one of the most photographed homes in Johnstown. The flood had hurled this tree through the house like a javelin. The six family members who were in the house all survived.

remembered stories of Benjamin Ruff's shoddy repairs. They remembered hearing that the discharge pipes were gone and that fish screens blocked the spillway.

Reporters wanted to know the flood's cause, too. They went to see the failed dam. Lake Conemaugh was gone. The exclusive clubhouse and lavish cottages sat untouched by the raging water that devastated Johnstown. The reporters heard about the fish screens and John Fulton's letter to Benjamin Ruff about the poor repairs.

"THE CLUB IS GUILTY," read the June 7 headline of the *New York World* newspaper.[3] The *New York Sun* declared, "CAUSE OF THE CALAMITY: The Pittsburgh Fishing Club

Chiefly Responsible." A *Chicago Herald* editorial was titled "Manslaughter or Murder?"[4]

Members of the South Fork Hunting and Fishing Club had vigorously protected their privacy at Lake Conemaugh. After the flood, a few members worked hard to help the relief effort. Some sent donations. Most members, though, remained silent. They did not want to be identified with the club. Donations from the club members for relief efforts ranged from $15 to Andrew Carnegie's $10,000. About thirty members gave nothing.

The club ceased to exist. Without lovely Lake Conemaugh, there was no reason for the members to go there.

Some Johnstown businessmen and families of victims sued. The club's lawyers claimed that the broken dam was not their fault. It burst, they said, because of the rain. They successfully argued the disaster was an "act of God." The South Fork Hunting and Fishing Club and its members were not found guilty of any negligence regarding the disaster.[5]

# CHAPTER 6

# The Future

The South Fork Dam, as it stood on May 31, 1889, was not adequate to contain Lake Conemaugh's water. Although the dam was originally well-built, alterations and repairs had not kept it at the same standards. Its safety features were compromised—the discharge pipes were gone and the spillway was smaller and blocked. Because of the poor repairs, the dam was weakest at its center. When the lake flowed over it, the dam failed. After the flood, the South Fork Dam was not rebuilt. The club was abandoned and eventually sold. The town of St. Michael was later built in part of the lakebed.

In Johnstown, the Cambria Iron Company mills were repaired and the steelworkers went back to work. New houses and stores soon lined the city streets. An opera house opened. Local baseball teams were soon cheered on new sports fields.

Gertrude Quinn's family stayed and built a new house and new store. Max McAchren lived the rest of his life in

Johnstown. Victor Heiser moved away. He eventually went on to medical school and became a public health doctor. Through his efforts to improve sanitation and his campaign against leprosy, he is credited with saving more than a million lives during his long career.

Johnstown residents took actions to try to prevent damage from future floods. They cleared the debris out of the rivers to widen and deepen their channels. They built flood walls to try to protect their city.[1]

In 1890, the Cambria Iron Company built an "inclined plane" up Johnstown's Yoder Hill. An inclined plane is a transportation device that uses cables to pull a tram car up tracks on a steep hillside. Passengers ride inside the tram car. The inclined plane provided access to a new city neighborhood, Westmount, on top of the hill. It would also help evacuate Johnstown in the event of future floods.

Johnstown was growing and prospering again. The city, though, had not seen its last flood.

On St. Patrick's Day, March 17, 1936, a severe rainstorm struck. In Johnstown, it poured for thirty-six hours. Deep snow in the Allegheny Mountains melted. Rivers surged out of their beds. Downtown, the water was seventeen feet deep. Four thousand people rode the inclined plane to safety. Twenty-five people died and $50 million in damage was done.[2]

In 1937, the federal government began a stream channelization project to protect Johnstown from future floods. The United States Army Corps of Engineers dug the river channels wider and deeper to hold more water. They poured concrete along them to prevent erosion. When the massive project was finished in 1943, Johnstown was celebrated as a "Flood Free City."

On July 20, 1977, a series of powerful storms assailed Johnstown. Twenty-one individual electrical storms settled over the region.[3] More than eleven inches of rain fell in just nine hours. People said that the pounding rain was so loud that they could barely hear the thunder from nearby bolts of lightning. The downpour was considered a "500-year event." This meant that experts believed there was

*T*his inclined plane (above) carried passengers, horses, wagons and, later, cars out of the center of Johnstown in subsequent floods.

only one chance in 500 that it would happen in any year.[4]

On Main Street, the water ran seven feet deep. The Army Corps of Engineers said that it would have been higher than the 1936 flood if not for the river channelization project. In downtown Johnstown, no lives were lost in the 1977 flood. However, nearby neighborhoods and communities were not so lucky.

An aerial view of the damage caused in Tanneryville by the 1977 flood.

Several earthen dams around Johnstown burst in the deluge. Investigators did not blame the design, construction, or maintenance of any of these dams. Still, the consequences in one town were tragic.

"The dam broke and it just took house after house," said one resident of Tanneryville, a town just west of Johnstown.[5] The Laurel Run Dam failed at about four in the morning. More water than had been in Lake Conemaugh was released.[6]

Many people were stuck in their homes. The violent storm made it difficult for them to leave to seek shelter elsewhere. Flood warnings did not alert residents to the impending danger. Forty-one people died in Tanneryville.

Dam failure was not to blame in nearby Seward. There was just too much water. "The windows were smashing and glass was flying, but we got the door open and got my wife out," Bobby Newman said, recalling his family's escape from their mobile home.[7] The Newmans lived in Hoover Trailer Park in Seward.

The city of Johnstown in 2001. When the South Fork Dam failed in 1889, the wall of water crashed into Johnstown through the gap in the mountains visible in the center of the picture.

"We floated down the river and I grabbed a tree and Gloria was holding onto my neck. Johnny grabbed the same tree and Bob got hold of one nearby. We just hung on and it started getting light and then three trailers blew up in the park. At the time, I thought it was the whole town. As we were hanging on the tree something came down the current and knocked our tree down and the three of us were afloat again— me, my wife, and Johnny. Bob still was hanging in his tree as we were washed away."[8]

All four members of the Newman family survived. After the water blasted through the trailer park, only two mobile homes there were standing. Nine people in Seward perished. Altogether, seventy-seven people died in Johnstown's 1977 flood.

*A*fter the 1889 flood, one woman saved some floodwater and sealed it in a bottle. The bottle of water is shown here on display at the Johnstown Flood Museum.

"A flood is better off on the pages of history books," wrote Larry Hudson, editor of the *Johnstown Tribune Democrat*, after the 1977 flood. "There are some things that the history books never told us. . . . They never told us how much it would hurt. Nothing about the birds singing as the dead lay heaped. . . . They never told us about the lumps in our throats, the knots in our stomachs, the sudden realization that we really did love a city."[9]

Two museums commemorate Johnstown's floods. The Johnstown Flood National Memorial is located above the remains of the South Fork Dam. The Memorial has a visitors' center, interpretive paths, and exhibits. Fifteen miles downstream is the Johnstown Flood Museum. Exhibits and an Academy Award-winning documentary explore the causes and consequences of the 1889 flood. The museum also celebrates the unbreakable spirit of Johnstown's people, who rebuilt their city and their lives.

| DATE | PLACE | TYPE OF DISASTER | DEATHS |
|---|---|---|---|
| September 8, 1900 | Galveston, TX | Hurricane winds and tidal wave | +6,000 |
| June 14, 1903 | Hippner, OR | Flooding | 325 |
| March 26, 1913 | Ohio and Indiana | Flooding on the Ohio River | 467 |
| June 3, 1921 | Pueblo, CO | Arkansas River overflows | 200 |
| March 12, 1928 | Santa Paula, CA | Collapse of St. Francis Dam | 450 |
| January 22, 1937 | Ohio and Mississippi | Flooding of Ohio and Mississippi river valleys | 250 |
| January 18–26, 1969 | Southern California | Floods and mudslides | 100 |
| August 17, 1969 | Mississippi Coast | Hurricane Camille pushes wall of water ashore | 256 |
| February 26, 1972 | Man, WV | Heavy rains cause dam collapse | 118 |
| June 9, 1972 | Rapid City, SD | Collapse of two dams | 263 |
| July 31, 1976 | Colorado | Flood on Big Thompson River | 139 |
| Summer, 1993 | Midwestern United States | Flooding on the Mississippi River | 51 |
| December 1996 | West Coast | Severe floods in California, Oregon, Washington, Idaho, Nevada, and Montana | 36 |

# Chapter Notes

### Chapter 1. A Dangerous Proposition

1. Gertrude Quinn Slattery, *Johnstown and its Flood* (Philadelphia: The Dorrance Press, 1936), p. 26.

2. Ibid., p. 25.

3. David McCullough, *The Johnstown Flood* (New York: Simon and Schuster, Inc., 1968), p. 150.

4. Slattery, p. 26.

5. Ibid.

6. Ibid., p. 27.

### Chapter 2. The Dam in the Mountains

1. David McCullough, *The Johnstown Flood* (New York: Simon and Schuster, Inc., 1968), p. 53.

2. Ibid., p. 54.

3. Nathan Daniel Shappee, *A History of Johnstown and the Great Flood of 1889: A Study of Disaster and Rehabilitation* (Doctoral Dissertation, University of Pittsburgh, 1940), p. 185.

4. McCullough, p. 56.

5. Ibid., p. 73.

6. Ibid., p. 74.

### Chapter 3. Prepare for the Worst

1. David McCullough, *The Johnstown Flood* (New York: Simon and Schuster, Inc., 1968), p. 90.

2. Anwei Skinsnes Law, *The Great Flood: Johnstown, Pennsylvania, 1889* (Johnstown Area Heritage Association, 1997), p. 27.

3. McCullough, p. 100.

4. Law, p. 45.

5. McCullough, p. 114.

### Chapter 4. "The End of the World"

1. Victor Heiser, *An American Doctor's Odyssey* (New York: W.W. Norton and Company, 1936), p. 4.

2. Gertrude Quinn Slattery, *Johnstown and its Flood* (Philadelphia: The Dorrance Press, 1936), p. 28.

3. Ibid., p. 31.

4. Ibid., p. 34.

5. Heiser, p. 7.

6. George Swank, "Our Calamity," *Johnstown Tribune*, June 14, 1889, p. 1.

7. J. J. McLaurin, *The Story of Johnstown* (Harrisburg, Pa.: James M. Place, 1890), p. 220.

8. Slattery, p. 49.

## Chapter 5. Relief and Recovery

1. Anwei Skinsnes Law, *The Great Flood: Johnstown, Pennsylvania, 1889* (Johnstown Area Heritage Association, 1997), p. 72.

2. Nathan Daniel Shappee, *A History of Johnstown and the Great Flood of 1889: A Study of Disaster and Rehabilitation* (Doctoral Dissertation, University of Pittsburgh, 1940), p. 307.

3. David McCullough, *The Johnstown Flood* (New York: Simon and Schuster, Inc., 1968), p. 246.

4. Law, p. 81.

5. Ibid., p. 83.

## Chapter 6. The Future

1. U. S. Army Corps of Engineers, Pittsburgh District, "Johnstown Flooding and the U.S. Army Corps of Engineers," *Johnstown, Pa. Local Flood Protection Project*, June 9, 1999, <http://www.lrp.usace.army.mil/fc/bjohn.htm> (March 20, 2002).

2. Ibid.

3. Larry Hudson, "The Places," *Johnstown Tribune Democrat*, August 19, 1977, p. 34.

4. U. S. Army Corps of Engineers, Pittsburgh District.

5. Ted Potts, "Tanneryville," *Johnstown Tribune Democrat*, August 19, 1977, p. 38.

6. "Once in Ten Thousand Years," *Johnstown Pennsylvania Information Source Online*, n.d., <http://www.johnstownpa.com/History/hist21.html> (March 20, 2002).

7. Robert Sefick, "How the Bobby Newmans Survived: Families Tell Tales of Horror," *Johnstown Tribune Democrat*, August 19, 1977, p. 29.

8. Ibid.

9. Edwin L. Hutcheson, *Floods of Johnstown 1889, 1936, 1977* (Johnstown, Pa.: Cambria County Tourist Council, Inc.), p. 29.

**Commissary**—A place where food supplies are distributed.

**Debris**—The remains of broken things. Wreckage, rubble.

**Discharge Pipes**—Outlet pipes. Pipes that allowed water to be released from the reservoir behind the dam.

**Engineer**—(1) A person trained in the science of designing and building certain projects including dams, roads, bridges, and machinery; (2) A person who runs a railroad engine or locomotive.

**Morgue**—A place where dead bodies are kept while awaiting identification or burial.

**Negligence**—Failure to use reasonable care.

**Pandemonium**—A place of wild disorder, noise, and confusion.

**Spillway**—A passageway to carry off excess water around a dam.

**Telegraph**—A communicating device that uses Morse Code to send messages.

**Undertaker**—A person who prepares the dead for burial.

# Further Reading

Bredeson, Carmen. *The Mighty Midwest Flood: Raging Rivers.* Berkeley Heights, N.J.: Enslow Publishers, Inc., 1999.

Gallagher, Jim. *The Johnstown Flood.* Philadelphia, Pa.: Chelsea House, 2000.

Gross, Virginia T. *The Day It Rained Forever: A Story of the Johnstown Flood.* New York: Penguin Putnam, Inc., 1993.

Law, Anwei Skinsnes. *The Great Flood.* Johnstown, Pa.: Johnstown Area Heritage Association, National Park Service, 1997.

Walker, Paul R. *Head for the Hills! The Amazing True Story of the Johnstown Flood.* New York: Random House, 1995.

# Internet Addresses

**Johnstown Area Heritage Association and the Johnstown Flood Museum**
http://www.jaha.org/flood/main.htm

**Johnstown Flood National Memorial, National Park Service**
http://www.nps.gov/jofl/home.htm

**A Quick Tour of the City of Johnstown, Pennsylvania**
http://ctcnet.net/gdsbm/city/city.htm#flood

**Teaching with Historic Places Lesson Plan, National Park Service**
http://www.cr.nps.gov/nr/twhp/wwwlps/lessons/5johnstown/5johnstown.htm